THE FALL & RISE OF THE CAVAN & LEITRIM

by Darragh Connol

GW00373904

Published by Mainline & Maritime Ltd
3 Broadleaze, Upper Seagry, near Chippenham, SN15 5EY
Tel: 07770 748615
www.mainlineandmaritime.co.uk
orders@mainlineandmaritime.co.uk
Printed in the UK
ISBN: 978-1-900340-76-2

Front Cover 6T en route from Dromod near Dereen in March 1959.

Colour Rail

Back Cover History at Dromod with two complete locomotives beside each other on 30th March 2019, NANCY and DROMAD are seen side by side, the first time they have been reunited for over 20 years. DROMAD was whisked away to the UK on the lowloader NANCY came on and is pending overhaul currently. See all our happy volunteers!

C&L Archive

Above An unusual view, taken from the footplate of 2L at Drumshanbo looking towards Arigna, taken in 1955.

John Wiltshire courtesy Peter Brabham

The history of the Cavan and Leitrim Railway has been covered by many sources, this book aims to have a closer look at the final years of the C&L as a railway, providing public accounts of the build up to closure and memories to recreate the scenes of that time. It also aims to continue through the gap from closure to the re-opening of the present railway at Dromod and the magnificent work carried out there.

By way of background, there had been many proposals for a railway through Leitrim, including overtures by local landowners to the Midland, Great Western Railway, eventually the "Cavan, Leitrim & Roscommon Light Railway & Tramway Co. Ltd" was formed on 3rd December 1883 to construct a 3ft gauge line from Belturbet through Ballyconnell, Ballinamore and Mohill to Dromod, with a branch from Ballinamore through Drumshanbo and Arigna to Boyle, encapsulating 48 ½ miles in total. The line linked the then already existing broad gauge railways, of the Great Northern Railway's Belturbet branch in the North East with the Midland, Great Western at Dromod in the South. The capital was to be raised by a Baronial Guarantee in the counties served, with most coming from Leitrim, but as the Roscommon Grand Jury withdrew its support the branch did not continue beyond Arigna and the "Roscommon" was dropped from the company's title.

The main line was opened for goods on 17th October 1887 and for passengers on 24th October 1887 while the branch opening followed on 2nd May 1888. Most people believe the Cavan and Leitrim's primary justification for existence was coal, but this was not the case. It was built mostly for cattle and fair traffic to transport cattle from the midlands to the ports of Belfast and Sligo for onward travel. It is also of note that the extension to the mines at Arigna itself, was not constructed until 2nd June 1920, the all-important extension from Arigna station to the mines at Derreenavoggy and Aughabehy was opened by the Board of Trade during the period of Governmental control of railways. This was constructed using the "defence against the realms act." It was proposed several times over the years, with funding being provided by the Government, however local opposition against the Mine Company prevented the extension.

In the early 1900's there was an ambitious proposal for a coast to coast narrow gauge railway which proposed the construction of a 3ft gauge line linking the then existing systems along the borders of Ulster, namely linking the Newry and Bessbrook Tramway with the Clogher Valley Railway, with a further extension to the Cavan & Leitrim Railway. This proposal also included a completely new stretch of railway, 110 miles in length, from Dromod on the Cavan & Leitrim to Clifden in County Galway. In addition to the main line, a 1900 Act of Parliament authorised the construction of a branch along the Dundalk, Newry and Greenore Railway to Greenore. At the time the DN&GR was agreeable to making its line between Newry and Greenore dual-gauged by laying down a third rail to enable narrow gauge trains to get to the quays at Greenore. The scheme came to naught for the country they passed through was mainly thinly populated agricultural land.

In 1903 Parliament authorised the building of a line from Maguiresbridge on the Clogher Valley to meet the C&L at Bawnboy Road station. The Act also authorised the amalgamation of the C&L, the CVR and the Newry Tramway to form a single company with the title of the Ulster & Connaught Light Railway but also provided for a four mile extension from the Arigna branch of the C&L to the Leitrim Coalfield, the acquisition of certain mining rights in the latter, and the building of a two mile extension from Dromod to Rooskey Lock on the River Shannon. The Rooskey extension was planned by the C&L but never received parliamentary approval. It is interesting to speculate what would have become of it, had it been built.

Post amalgamation into the Great Southern Railways, the line became a dumping ground for other locomotives, and rolling stock, from other lines as they eventually closed down. There seemed to be a Munster invasion in this part of the North West, with Cork, Blackrock and Passage and Tralee and Dingle Light Railway locos, wagons and carriages all descending on the railway at various periods throughout the GSR and CIE reign. At the very end the line was the last steam only outpost on Irish Railways, the only internal combustion engine at the end was a former Tralee and Dingle Light Railway inspection railcar that was based on the West Clare. The Cavan and Leitrim had an independent streak and this showed right to the end. Many accounts (as featured) depict a decrepit, decaying and dismal end to the Cavan and Leitrim, with photographs showing locomotives and carriages falling apart and in horrendous condition, it must have been an incredible sight to witness.

Acknowledgements

Thanks must be made firstly to Iain McCall who kindly facilitated the publication of this book. Thanks is extended to the Anglo-Celt who kindly gave us permission to use their newspaper publications, without which there would be nothing. Several enthusiasts have also given permission to use photographs of the C&L, we would like to specifically thank the Bluebell Railway Museum Archive for providing the J. J. Smith images, Richard Barber of the ARPT, Ciaran Cooney of the Irish Railway Record Society, Michael Whitehouse and others who are named within the text.

An interpretation of the Cavan and Leitrim Railway Company crest, post removal of Roscommon!

C&L Archive

A JOURNEY ON THE C&L: A FAREWELL CAMEO BY H. E. VICKERS

Listowel and Ballybunnion, Ballymena and Larne, Cork, Blackrock and Passage, Tralee and Dingle, Cavan and Leitrim, what wonderful rolling titles the small Irish lines had. As we sped along from Mullingar behind our buzzing diesel I wondered what the sole unchanged survivor of these would be like. Would it show the depressing routine of rotting sleepers, peeling paintwork, derelict buildings, a daily decrepit train?

Dromod station building as of March 1959.
H Stevenson

CBPR loco 12L is seen at Dromod with the "Bus coach" 7L ready to depart.

Colour Rail

CBPR loco 10L on the turntable at Dromod on 5th August 1958.

The waiting "train" at Dromod sprang the first surprise, a modern bus-type carriage, painted a rather drab grey, and similar to those built at Inchicore for the West Clare line. Next was the sound of busy shunting down the yard, caused by an ex Cork, Blackrock and Passage 2-4-2T No. 12, absolutely filthy from end to end. Her driver scowled at my official footplate pass; they didn't hold with such things around here, but nevertheless I could come with them if I liked, provided I put some proper clothes on. This done we got the "right away" and were off to Ballinamore. That poor engine! It was in a terrible state, filthy inside as well as out,

with spill oil cans littering the cab, driving wheels rubbing holes in the boiler sheeting as we rolled (as far as I could tell in the boiler too), reversing gear snatching fit to burst, and a regulator handle falling off its spindle. Rolling on at a fair 20-25 m.p.h,. the driver confided that he once had a train here at a calculated 50 m.p.h. Admittedly he had a "little drink" but thanks to the great reliability of his guard and his accurate watch, the punishment had been confined to a week's holiday – at his own expense. I was glad to be on the morning train.

12L seen at Ballinamore with a Dromod bound service, the condition of the loco is horrendous.

Colour Rail

12L crossing a T&D loco at Mohill, note the "bus carriage" 7L on the left.

Colour Rail

At Mohill, we crossed a Tralee and Dingle 2-6-0T on an "up" coal special and there followed some bad tempered shunting of our 18 odd trucks. It seemed the Tralee and Dingle engine had not stayed to help as had been arranged. Then we were off again, to stop immediately on the steep gradients across the main road. The driver had remembered to collect the train staff. On once again it was a comfort that head-on collision had not featured in Cavan and Leitrim history, so far as I knew.

The course of the line was interesting, but not outstanding, until we descended the stiff bank into Ballinamore and the Arigna branch swept up and round to meet us before we made an unexpected and imposing side by side entrance into the junction and headquarters of the line. As we passed it the home signal came off.

Straight on to Belturbet after lunch, by the same train, but with a different crew. Lashings of coal were put on at infrequent intervals and we groaned and grunted over the tops of the many banks at a walking pace with full regulator and nominal mid-gear. No wonder the wretched engine was falling to bits. The track was very rough and even the fireman noticed one series of memorable rolls. Prolonged shunting at Ballyconnell and a fill of water, then on again to Belturbet past country still strangely undistinguished in spite of its numerous lakes and hills.

6T seen en-route to Dromod after taking on water at Ballyconnell on 28th March 1959, with a goods train Belturbet with a good train.
H. Emulus - ARPT

Another surprise here, a GNR 0-6-0 was fetching a truck of cattle on the broad gauge, although the line had been officially closed to all traffic at least six months previously! The station was depressingly deserted and so I watched our No. 12 shunting and turning, while her safety valves blew fit to burst. The Ballinamore men never appeared fuel conscious and their charges blew off by the hour. Back to Ballinamore with the friendly guard in the composite; sitting on the lighting batteries the riding was much better but still lively. The bus type body was obviously not suited to railway treatment and the panels were badly battered in the van section.

Next morning round the sheds, to find no less than six locomotives in steam that day, one on the mainline (No. 12), one on the branch (Tralee and Dingle 2-6-0T), and the rest on the Arigna coal "specials" (the remaining Tralee and Dingle tanks, including the 2-6-2T and the Cavan and Leitrim 4-4-0Ts). All were on their last legs, like No. 12.

An unidentified CBPR loco at Bawnboy Road in an undated scene, most likely 12L.

J Philips

I travelled to Arigna later, in the original American type "caboose" composite as the driver declined to honour my footplate pass – "no room". The Cavan and Leitrim was run by men from Ballinamore and not by bits of paper from Dublin. Leaving our freight at Drumshanbo, the 2-6-0T took our carriage to Arigna alone, where her crew nearly got stuck on an unbalanced turntable. Returning to Drumshanbo she picked up some 18 cattle trucks which taxed her powers noisily on the tortuous and switchback road home. Some excitement at the road crossing as we and a tractor just managed to stop short of each other with brakes and tyres screeching, and with a final and exhilarating burst of speed we rattled over the lower level crossing at Ballinamore and panted ever more slowly round the town and up into the station.

The return to Dromod through the cold March twilight, on No 12 again, was sheer delight. She had a third crew, this time on their mettle with a long, mixed train. Our 4ft 6in driving wheels stalked the banks with a raucous dignity and the stealthy exhaust echoed clearly across the fields and hedges – glorious music indeed. No restricted cut-offs this time, but everything she had. The shining rails guided us through the gathering dusk, past the barren rock-strewn hills and lakes, until they too disappeared, and scattered level crossing lights were our only guide. I was now quite lost in a strange countryside, lit only by the glare from our fire and the occasional flash from a dropping cinder, until at long last a "green" high up in the trees, and far away to one side told us we were curving into Mohill.

A ten minute blow up for a winded engine and then we were on our way again with a rising, frosty moon for company – there was a main line connection to make. Scattered lights ahead, another "green", a left hand turn, and we were back at Dromod all too soon. In the warmth of the slick Sligo bound diesel buffet car, aided by a welcome glass of Guinness, I filed a memory of a grand little line of character, one of the few which have been allowed to work themselves really hard to their allotted end, and which remained uncompromisingly loyal to steam, a veritable oasis in a strange new diesel world. My one and only visit to the Cavan and Leitrim had come to its end.

3T in the evening sunlight on the Arigna Tramway, in March 1959, not long left to go

Colour Rail

A FRIENDLY LINE

The line was referred to as friendly and very much serving the locality from which it passed, Councillor Joe Mooney referred to this in an article in the "Leitrim Guardian" marking the 100th anniversary in 1988;

When I was growing up in our house, "The Railway Bar" [Drumshanbo], was the port of call for those who wanted a drink to quench their thirst after arrival, or "give us a quick one, before the train goes" as they were running for it! Particularly before leaving for Ballinamore, the train waiting at the platform and would-be passengers had a view of it from the whole length of Church Street, or to give it its more ancient name, Carricknabrack, so that those who were having their "deoch an dorais" had a good view from the Bridge Bar (Earleys), Frank Earleys, The Railway Hotel (Cooneys) and our house. But if they didn't happen to see the train, good enough of the engine driver, he blew the whistle, but it wasn't the departure whistle, and as a result passengers emanated from the various houses, not necessarily all public houses! However those in our house, and in Cooneys opposite, took their time, because they knew the train would wait for those further down the street. But how did they know? Perhaps the ones coming up the street knew the train couldn't go without the driver, or maybe the fireman!

8L is seen at Drumshanbo on an Arigna service on 24th September 1951, note the desolate platform. Note the carriage still carries faded GSR crimson.

Bluebell Railway Museum Archive

HOPE FOR SURVIVAL

Towards the mid to late 1950's news of the Electricity Supply Board's decision to commission a power plant on the shores of Lough Allen was announced, this led to speculation and rumours of closure. A blessing came in the form of a new coal contract from Irish Cement, which was to revitalise the C&L and kept the line going to the bitter end. Irish Rail Fans "Fuel and Fair Traffic on the Cavan and Leitrim Railway" (Volume 3, 1957, Number 2) reported this,

The small towns served by the Cavan & Leitrim Railway are noted principally for the active part played by them in the cattle trade of Ireland and it is evident that this fact was uppermost in the minds of the promoters who, in 1883, campaigned to link Mohill, Ballinamore, Drumshanbo and Ballyconnell with the MGWR at Dromod and with the GNR(I) at Belturbet. Seventy years after the opening of the "main line", livestock traffic still plays no small part in its struggle for existence. Nevertheless, today it is to the branch - the line from Ballinamore to Arigna - that the system primarily looks for the traffic which is its very life-blood - coal!

In this undated view, 2L on a coal train is viewed from the brake van.
Ernie's Railway Archive

Since the end of the Second World War, bringing with it a subsequent restoration of supplies of British coal, there has been a diminishing demand for the 'soft' Arigna product and with the termination of a contract to supply the sugar factories of CSÉ (*Comhlacht Suicra Eireann- Irish Sugar Company*) and a series of strikes at the mines, spasms of inactivity have recurred ever more frequently. Although during these periods the daily mixed train to Arigna usually worked some wagons of coal along with the ordinary goods traffic of the line, the "Paths for Coal Trains" provided in the working timetable were infrequently utilised.

6T is seen at the pit head at Derreenavoggy in 1957, 6T had recently arrived and looks relatively clean by C&L standards. The bunkers are centre left, note the aerial ropeway above.

J Philips

C&L 4-4-0T 3L seen at Arigna station with a loaded coal train ready to depart

Colour Rail

Since September 1956 a new contract has been secured with Cement Ltd for the supply of Arigna coal to their factories. When this traffic first commenced it was destined for Drogheda factory and thus regular coal specials ran for the first time over the Ballinamore-Belturbet section to be transhipped at the latter point into the standard gauge wagons of the GNR for the rest of the journey. At the end of February 1957 the flow of coal was diverted to Dromod whence it is railed by CIÉ to Limerick for the Castlemungret cement factory. Despite the fact that the future of the C&L lies in the extent of its coal traffic, it is gratifying to record that the carriage of cattle which brought the line into being is still of considerable value. A two-way outlet is afforded by the connections at Belturbet towards Belfast and at Dromod towards Dublin so that cattle sold at the local fairs can be sent to either port, although in practice almost all of the traffic is sent via Belturbet. The exception is Mohill fair, from which some Dublin bound wagons are despatched but, even so, the greater proportion is railed north. Mohill fairs are the largest on the system and in particular those in October and February - the latter is for some unaccountable reason known as "Monaghan Fair" - generally tax the railway's resources to the utmost. By way of illustration the following account of the February 1957 fair traffic may be of interest.

6T with convertible wagon at Belturbet, nearing the end, on 28th March 1959.

H. Emulus – ARPT

Monday February 25th 1957 dawned fine and sunny as the 08:00 mixed set off from Ballinamore for Dromod. The train was headed by ex CB&PR loco 12L and comprised coach 21L and van 22L - both ex T&D vehicles transferred to the C&L in 1954 - together with 6 empty cattle wagons bound for Mohill to augment the supply of wagons stocked there since the previous Saturday. At 09:10 the first empty cattle special left Ballinamore for Mohill, followed by three similar further specials between then and 11:00. A train of coal empties, headed by loco 8L, also slipped quietly away from Ballinamore during the morning bound for Arigna to cater for the morrow's output from the mines. Ballinamore

had then relapsed into a sunny somnolence - which was more apparent than real - when the telephone's strident clangour at 13:00 announced the departure from Mohill of the return mixed working from Dromod. Loco 12L made good time with the train of passenger coach, van and 11 wagons of stock, for, despite this load, she was only 11 minutes late into Ballinamore and lost only another 3½ minutes over the remaining section of the journey to Belturbet. At this latter terminus the wagons of stock were quickly shunted into the transfer bank where standard gauge GNR wagons were standing in readiness.

Ballinamore looking south on 27th June 1957, with the mainline to Dromod on the left and the Arigna branch to the right, the physical junction between these routes was located at the station and they ran parallel as seperate routes beyond here. Note the CBPR loco 12L has a rake of empty coal wagons and two former T&D carriages in tow, composite 21L and brake 22L.

Bluebell Railway Museum Archive

Before the return of this regular train at 16:15 to Ballinamore the first of the loaded cattle specials from Mohill arrived at Belturbet. It was headed by the other CB&PR loco - 10L - and comprised 12 wagons and van. On its arrival loco 12L returned westwards with the 16:15 to await crossing the next cattle special from Mohill at Ballyconnell. After half an hour's wait, loco 5T at last arrived hauling 9 wagons of stock to allow the regular to proceed further west to Bawnboy Road where another wait was expected. This did not arise, however, as the third cattle special was held at Ballinamore to avoid further delay to the returning mixed train. Before 19:00 a fourth and final cattle special from Mohill passed through Ballinamore hauled by loco 3T just in time to clear the road for the departure of the 19:00 Ballinamore-Dromod regular train behind loco 8L.

Thus ended a day of intensive activity on this, the last remaining steam operated narrow gauge railway in Ireland. Few lovers of Irish railways will hesitate to join with us in hoping that the fascinating Cavan & Leitrim may as expeditiously handle these coal and "Monaghan Fair" specials, in addition to its regular traffic, for many years to come.

It is interesting to note that the above surge in coal traffic required additional motive power on an already

overstretched situation in the North West. At the time there was a lack of other suitable replacements. The West Clare section having condemned steam motive power from 1955, due to replacement of steam with the new diesel Walker units. Inchicore had some 3ft steam locos awaiting scrapping, of these former Tralee and Dingle Light Railway 2-6-0T 6T was reprieved and sent North West. It is interesting that this loco was the most travelled of all of CIE's locomotives having operated on the Tralee and Dingle, the West Clare and the Cavan and Leitrim. Her overhaul was also reported by Irish Rail Fans (Volume 3, 1957, number 4), Loco 6T which recently underwent a complete overhaul in Inchicore works as reported in our last issue was sent to the Cavan & Leitrim section at the beginning of July bringing the stud of locos now at Ballinamore to its highest ever total of 10. The additional loco was required on the line to assist in handling heavy coal traffic from the Arigna mines, which in recent months has reached such proportions as to require the running of 4 special coal trains daily in each direction on the Arigna Tramway in addition to the one mixed train. Two of these specials run from Arigna to Belturbet with coal for Drogheda cement factory, while the other two run to Dromod with coal for the cement factory at Castlemungret, Co. Limerick.

6T at Dromod approaching turntable in 1957, still looking somewhat clean.

Ernie's Railway Archive

It is known that while 6T was renovated for the C&L, it had some steaming issues and leaked steam through the smokebox. The C&L engine crew were nifty and discovered a way to resolve this by putting scraw in the floor of the smokebox over a hole, this seemingly did the trick and 6T worked fine. Despite the steaming issues 6T was pushed hard from 1957 and beyond bearing the brunt of coal specials, it also recorded history with the last 12:20 service from Dromod, and the last passenger train from Castlegregory (on the Tralee and Dingle) 20 years previously, in 1939. She was also most accident prone on the Tralee and Dingle, featuring in numerous accident reports, however she settled down on the Cavan and Leitrim.

CLOSURE BECKONS

The optimism from the cement contract was not to last too long, closure had been mooted previously for the C&L as early as 1939, C.I.E. reported severe losses on the route and intended to close the line. There was of course opposition locally, this was shown in "Leitrim to Fight Rail Closure" (Anglo Celt, 19 March 1959).

Traders in three Leitrim towns plan to call a boycott of C.I.E road freight services if the Cavan and Leitrim rail service is closed down, as announced on April 1. The traders will refuse to accept goods delivered by C.I.E lorries and will return them to senders, if the boycott plan goes through.

Some traders have already sent back goods delivered by road with the request: "please send them again – by rail". Said one Trader "we are witnessing not only the death of a railway line but the death of all South Leitrim because this was our principal industry, lifeline and hope for future development and survival." If the lines go Co. Leitrim will be without a rail service since the Sligo, Leitrim and Northern Counties Railway which served North Leitrim has already been closed. Buses and C.I.E road freight vehicles are to replace trains.

6T is seen shunting at Dromod in February, 1959.

National Library Ireland

Mr. Patrick Martin, Chairman of Ballinamore and District Trader's Association, leading the last-ditch fight to save the railway said "Even if it is closed it will not be the end of the fight because traders may refuse to accept goods delivered by C.I.E lorries. If C.I.E would cooperate with the traders of Ballinamore, Mohill and Drumshanbo it would make all the difference but the company has never assisted us to bring traffic to the railway".

Opened in 1887:
The narrow gauge line, opened in 1887 for the Cavan, Leitrim and Roscommon Light Railway and Tramway Co., runs from Belturbet to Dromod through Mohill, Ballinamore and Ballyconnell along with another arm from Ballinamore through Drumshanbo to the Arigna coal mines over a total distance of about 34 miles.

Traders allege that C.I.E and the G.S.R let the railway die. When the G.S.R took over, carriage sheds at Ballinamore were dismantled and sold. Since then the carriages have been left out in the open and many have rotted away. Local people allege that the line was run with "ancient" passenger carriages and rolling stock.

A carriage is seen rotting at Ballinamore yard, on the site of the carriage shed, it was a very short sighted move by the GSR to remove the structure and led to the decay of the carriage fleet.

Armstrong - ARPT

CIE view:

C.I.E. say the line is being closed to save a loss of £40,000 a year. But a special "railway closing" Road grant of £40,000 has been made by the Government to Leitrim Co. Council this year and is to continue for at least five years. Local traders say the loss was inflated by C.I.E. waste and inefficiency, the running of needless services and the "pirating" of rail service by the C.I.E road freight services.

Since January 1 last, Arigna coal, which was the mainstay of the service for many years has been switched from rail to road transport. The traders allege that, in order to take the traffic away from the railway, C.I.E. gave special freight rates equal to rail transport rate. They say that the arrangement is being subsidised by C.I.E. and the state to pave the way for closing of the line which has an extension to special pithead sidings.

Local traders allege a deliberate and persistent C.I.E. campaign to take traffic away from the line. They say that goods consigned to Ballinamore were re-routed to Carrick-on-Shannon and hauled over 16 miles of road by C.I.E lorries to bypass the Dromod-Ballinamore line. Goods consigned to Drumshanbo traders have also been sent to Carrick-on-Shannon to await delivery by the twice a week C.I.E. goods lorry service though there is a daily service, they say.

Derreenavoggy bunkers in February 1959, note the aerial ropeway which linked to the pitheads.

National Library Ireland

Mr. J. Mooney, a member of Leitrim Co. Council and son of one of the directors of the old Cavan and Leitrim Railway said: "The line has survived in spite of C.I.E. for many years. This is South Leitrim's main industry, though it is costing the state money to keep it going. But thousands are being thrown around on all sides to attract foreign industrialists, protect home industries and subsidise the production of agricultural and manufactured goods here that could be imported at much less cost to the State and the consumer."

West Clare Line:

Traders point out that the West Clare narrow gauge line was dieselised six years ago. C.I.E. promised to dieselise the Cavan and Leitrim line if the experiment proved successful. But the promise was not kept. Plans for a new industry at Ballinamore employing up to 20 at the start and with a peak employment of 100, may be jeopardised by the closure of the line, said Mr. W. P. Toolan, the Ballinamore solicitor who is secretary of the local committee which is raising £5,000 for the project: "One of the amenities which we held forth for the purpose of enticing industrialists to come here was the fact that we were served by a railway. Now that this closure is being forced on us we find that we are severely prejudiced in our discussions with industrialists."

Leitrim Co. Council will lose £489 rates paid by the railway, Ballinamore will lose a weekly payroll of £400. Over 100 employees will be uprooted and their families will be uprooted and sent elsewhere. Leitrim's population has already fallen from 52,000 to 37,000 since 1921.

The closure of the line went ahead as planned by C.I.E. like so many other rural Irish branches of that time. However, the C&L was the last steam-only outpost on C.I.E. and the last steam only narrow gauge line on the island (The County Donegal and West Clare having railcars and diesel locos). There was much publicity around this, with many enthusiasts flocking to the line. The Anglo Celt produced a superb feature on the line the week before and after closure, along with accounts by enthusiast groups.

"THE END OF THE LINE,
IT WAS A FAITHFUL FRIEND OF THE PEOPLE"

Cavan and Leitrim railway is passing into history by A.F Mc Entee (Anglo Celt, 28 March 1959)

When the 8:40pm train from Dromod steams into Ballinamore station at 9:45pm on Tuesday next March 31, the most friendly little railway system in all the world will have ceased to exist. Yes! It's the end of the line for the 72 years old Cavan and Leitrim Railway. Its uphill battle to avoid the axe of economy is over.

6T stands at the platform at Dromod on 28th March 1959, awaiting departure to Ballinamore.

H. Emulus - ARPT

Leitrim people everywhere, and indeed all those who have had the opportunity of even a passing acquaintance with the "narrow gauge" line will feel a sense of deep personal loss at the passing of a service which had become an integral part of the Irish way of life. It was the faithful friend of the people during a turbulent period in the country's history. Nowhere else, perhaps, more than in distant lands will the news of its requiem revive nostalgic memories. In most cases the little railway was the first contact with the outside world for the countless thousands who down the years were forced to emigrate from the Leitrim hills in order to obtain a livelihood.

As distinct from the mighty "Enterprise" with its helter-skelter race to beat the clock, here was a railway which, as it were, waited for the people – and at the same time kept better time than some of its bigger brothers. Like the "babbling brook" it meandered through the countryside making friends with the rural population before "sparkling out" to click-clack along the public road and keep company with its passing traffic. The whistle of the engine had to mean something to the inhabitants of the neat white-washed cottages that dot the area from one end of the line to the other. It was to them what Big Ben is to the Londoner.

On the same train as the previous picture, 6T is seen proceeding at Bawnboy.
H. Emulus - ARPT

For the little boy who became the envy of his school pals and achieved his life's ambition by "riding the engine"; the belated traveller for whom the train waited, and sometimes stopped; the railway fans who annually visited Leitrim "just to look at the trains"…these and a host of others will mourn the passing of a true friend.

To learn something about the men behind the scenes of this unique railway, and if possible to get a cross-section of views on its closure, I visited all the towns and stations on the line. Everywhere I went I found a deep rooted family tradition amongst the men of the railway and an inherent love of the railroad. Amongst the general public there was a genuine affection for a railway line that had given the better part of a generations service to the county.

Most railwaymen agreed that the closure had been inevitable. For them it meant, at the least, a transfer and a break with old ties. Their chief worry was that at the time of my visit there had been no official notification as to their future headquarters. There were mixed feelings amongst the business people on the question of closure. For some centres – Ballinamore in particular – the loss would be serious. In other areas the view was that if a good road service was substituted it would be some compensation, and this has been promised.

Ballinamore's big loss:
However, I was chiefly concerned with the personnel of the railroad. It was refreshing to meet and talk with the men who have directed the fortunes of the "Cavan and Leitrim" over the years. The neat, well-kept stations were an insight to the character of the occupants. The personal touch was in evidence everywhere, relieving that drabness that one usually associates with the railways. The title "Stationmaster" as applied to Leitrim was certainly a misnomer; "guardian", I thought, would have been a better word.

Ballinamore's works was a substantial affair with machines capable of undertaking complete loco repairs, post amalgamation the workshop's equipment was plundered by the G.S.R in the name of standardisation, but the Ballinamore men could still undertake repairs and full wagon rebuilds.

C&L Archive

CLR number 8 is seen on the turntable at Ballinamore surrounded by works staff, note we see a rare glimpse of the carriage shed in the background.

Leitrim Library

At Ballinamore, headquarters of the railway, where the old Board room of the original directors is still to be seen, the real tragedy of the lines closing was revealed. Stationmaster Paddy McNamara, a native of Kinsale, Co. Cork, six years at Ballinamore, told me that the weekly wages bill was about £450, rising at peak periods to £600.

It requires little imagination to realise what this loss will mean to Ballinamore with its 730 odd population. Since the line was established there have been six Stationmasters at headquarters. The five who served before McNamara were named McCoy, Sampson, McTeague, Cahill and Whelan. To Athlone born loco foreman, Dermot Spollen, who has in his possession the name plate of one of the first engines on the line – the "May", and to a cleaner John Joe Gallogy, of Lawderdale, I am indebted for a wealth of information on the history of the railway.

Ballinamore running shed with 3L, 2L & 8L in the engine shed, on 10th August 1956, no Kerry or Cork invaders here.

C&L Archive

Ballinamore with 8L undergoing attention, note the driving wheels have been removed for attention.

Armstrong – ARPT

Ballinamore with two Munster locos, former Tralee and Dingle, Kerr Stuart 2-6-0T 4T with an unidentified Cork Blackrock and Passage Railway loco undergoing work 1957.

National Library Ireland

Ballinamore sheds looking at 6T's cab on 28th March 1959.

H. Emulus – ARPT

Driver Paddy Rowley, married man, 46 years on the railway, gave an inkling of the difficulties confronting the workers during the fight for independence, a period during which the railways were used by the Black and Tans. He recalled an incident at Mohill station, when as fireman, he refused to man the engine because the train was conveying British troops. He was taken down the platform by the officer in charge and told; "my instructions are to shoot you". "Eventually they let me go" said Paddy. "It was the day of the Mohill fair and when the military left the station we brought the train to Ballinamore".

Cavan and Leitrim Number 8 "Queen Victoria" is seen at Dromod in 1924 with a service from Ballinamore. This was taken at an interesting time in Irish politics and Dromod had much activity during this period. The crew of 8 removed the nameplate and buried it at Ballinamore yard. The management discovered this and ordered it to be put back, then according to legend it was taken off again and thrown down a well on the Arigna branch, and was never seen again. The Ballinamore main also lined the loco in green white and orange, gaining the name the "Sinn Fein engine". The C&L enginemen were proud patriotic men, records show that an Irish tri-colour was fitted to a loco's smokebox and ran all the way from Belturbet to Dromod in 1918.

C&L Archive

Another link with the troubled times in Ireland was supplied by Mr. Hugh McKeon, retired railway guard, who resides with his wife at Railway Terrace, Ballinamore. He entered service as a checker at Dromod in 1910 and worked under three companies – the Cavan and Leitrim, G.S.R and C.I.E. He was arrested in Dromod by the Black and Tans in 1920 and interned in Ballykinlar until the signing of the treaty. His fellow prisoners included Mr. Sean Lemass, Minister for Industry and Commerce; Mr. Joseph McGrath, of the Irish Hospitals Trust; the late Dr. T. F. O'Higgins, T.D, the late district justice Louis J. Walsh; Mr. Peader Kearney, composer of the National Anthem; the late Mr. Sam Holt, T.D.; Carrick on Shannon; Mr. Sean O'Farrell; income tax Inspector, now living in Dublin; Mr. Paddy Dunne, propieter of the "Leitrim Observer", Mr. Paddy Flood, District Court Clerk, Ballinamore; the late Mr. Andrew Mooney, County Councillor.

Escape from death:
A few years after his release Mr. McKeon had a providential escape from death when a coal wagon became derailed at Kiltubrid station on the Drumshanbo-Ballinamore line. He was thrown from the guards van onto the rail, and the wagon heavily laden with Arigna coal, went over him. He was trapped for several hours until the coal was unloaded. Apart from severe crushing and facial injuries which required hospital treatment. Mr. McKeon was none the worse of his harrowing experience. It was during this period that the railway figured in an important legal action governing the liability of the company in the case of injury to a passenger travelling on an excursion ticket. The High Court held that Company were not liable.

An unusual view at Dromod transhipment platform with a 3ft gauge wagon on a broad gauge wagon, judging by the couplings it looks to be a former CBPR wagon chassis with Inchicore built body.

Leitrim Library

On his retirement from the railways in April last year Mr. McKeon was the recipient of a presentation from railway colleagues. My visit to Ballinamore coincided with the day of the monthly cattle fair. It was an unusually large fair, with hundreds of cattle and numerous buyers. Yet the railway did not get any additional business as a result of the fair. Out every road from Ballinamore I saw the heavy trucks being loaded with cattle. What a change from the old days when special trains would be needed to clear the cattle to the various destinations.

The "red dog of Drumshanbo":
A flash back to the good old days of cheap travel was provided at Drumshanbo by Stationmaster William Grogan and Foreman Tom Shanley who showed me the original dockets issued on September 6th 1888, for the carriage of one red dog and one horse from Drumshanbo to Belturbet.

For the dog the charge was sixpence and for the horse 8/-.

A native of Ballinahinch, Connemara, Stationmaster Grogan is five years in Drumshanbo and was previously at Crossdoney, County Cavan. His father before him worked on the old Midland Railways. His attitude to the closing of the line was philosophical "There is not much we can do about it. It may be a blessing in disguise". Foreman Shanley, whose father was also on the line before him, joined the railway in 1929. Eighty three years old Eddie Callery whom I interviewed in his well laid out comfortable esidence at Leitrim Hill, Drumcong, where he lives with his son and daughter, gave a lifetime of service to the Cavan and Leitrim Railway before he retired as driver 12 years ago. "I joined in the bad times when there was no eight hour day and no talk about unions" said Mr. Callery. "We had to work as long as were ordered to".

Drumshanbo on 14th March 1959 looking towards Arigna, note the GSR era bilingual sign

Bluebell Railway Museum Archive

3T is seen in this undated view at Drumshanbo.

C&L Archive

Mr. Callery, a native of Doogra, Roscommon, recalled with pleasure the occasion when he became the possessor of a pedal bicycle and was able to cycle the seven miles to his work in Drumshanbo at 6am each morning. "I was earning 12/- a week at that time" he laughed. Mr. Callery is certainly well qualified to give on opinion on the railways. His four brothers were all railwaymen and his father worked on the old Midland Great Western. His son John Joseph Callery, is a driver on the Cavan and Leitrim.

"I always prophesised that it would go sooner or later" he said in reply to my query. "In my young days everything and everybody had to go by train. The tide has turned now and with all the big lorries, vans and motor cars the people have not to rely on the railways. I am sorry to see it going. The whistle of the train gave us the time, and the railway gave good employment, but the world has changed – even the weather has changed, All we want is speed now" concluded this G.O.M of the railway. "Whoever lies for another twenty years will see more changes. The Aeroplanes will be very popular"

The halt at Arigna:

Across the lordly Shannon into Roscommon and along the shores of Lough Allen to Arigna Halt to meet the good-humoured Mrs. Annie Plunkett, mother of six children and a native of Ballinamore. Her husband is a railway employee in Mohill and Mrs. Plunkett has been halt keeper at Arigna for 10½ years.

Arigna station is seen here on 28th March 1959, with former T&D 2-6-2T 5T on charge of a one carriage consist and a party of enthusiasts.

H. Emulus - ARPT

Former T&D loco 3T on the mineral extension line in September 1957, this section was unique in that it had a mountainous terrain as a backdrop.

Ernie's Railway Archive

Standing in the shadow of Sliabh an Iarainn she stated; "The closing of the line is a big blow to us. I don't know what we will do yet. Once the coal stopped going by rail and the generating station opened it was the beginning of the end. I am afraid there is no future for the railway. During the emergency this was a very busy station with special trains carrying coal from Arigna to all parts." When asked to pose for a photograph Mrs. Plunkett laughingly replied "well I'm used to this anyway"; obviously referring to the many tourists who visit the area in search of photographic records of the narrow gauge.

5T is seen entering Ballinamore from Arigna with a coal special, note the Dromod line on left, these continued as separate lines until the station.

Ernie's Railway Archive

Mohill and Dromod:

Mohill Station holds what must be a record on the Cavan and Leitrim line by way of prizes won in best kept stations competition. In the eighteen years from 1940 to 1958 the station has secured three first prizes, six seconds, five thirds and four fourths. Certainly an impressive array. Leitrim-born station master Jim Flynn, who takes a natural pride in the charming appearance of the station epitomises everything that the railway stands for. A service of 35 years has not blunted his humour in any degree and his genial outlook is infectious. Expressing a genuine sorrow at the closing of the line he added "Bianconi has to make way for the railways, now the railways have to make way for something else. It is inevitable".

Kerr Stuart 4T is seen blasting through Mohill with an empty coal special in 1957.
Ernie's Railway Archive

4T is seen 2 years later taking on water at Mohill with a Dromod bound service.

J. Powell

At Dromod station, where the narrow gauge line reaches its most southernmost point and links up with the broad gauge, the Sligo to Dublin diesel train paused for a moment before resuming its headlong dash citywards, making a striking contrast to the leisurely shunting of the Cavan and Leitrim engine on the opposite platform. Here so to speak were the old and new. Dromod was the stopping off place for the railway fans who came year after year to travel on the "narrow gauge" to Arigna and back to Dromod in time for the Dublin connection. Stationmaster Michael Twomey, from Millstreet, West Cork has been five years in Dromod. "The Cavan and Leitrim was out of date" he stated, "and no business firm could justify the expenditure to bring it up to date." He added that they would miss the tourists who annually came to Dromod to get a connection with the "narrow gauge" line. While not knowing their names, they got to know them by their regular visits.

A view of Dromod platform on 14th March 1959 from the gate, showing 6T ready with the 12:20 Ballinamore service, note the crowds of enthusiasts, fortunately this platform still sees a steam service.

Bluebell Railway Museum Archive

Dromod yard viewed from a passenger train, it reversed to the goods loop to collect wagons, with passengers on board of course! Note you can see the loop for the station area, the siding for the engine shed and turntable, and another siding which led to the carriage shed, since torn down by the GSR. This view is almost identical 60 years later, however the preservation era company has re-instated the carriage shed!

C&L Archive

The Cavan Line:

At the other end of the line at Belturbet, I spoke to Halt Keeper Frank McKiernan, a native of Cavanagh, Ballyconnell. The station has been reduced to a Halt in recent years. Frank, who is 15 years with the Cavan and Leitrim, told me that there was still heavy goods traffic between the narrow and broad gauge. The people of Belturbet, he said, had been promised a good road service when the line closed. "It is going to be a big change for all of us" he added. "The broad line from here to Ballyhaise is also coming to an end, so that it will mean a complete closing down here".

6T is seen here on 28th March 1959, at the transhipment platforms at Belturbet, note the broad gauge GNR(I) van on the right.

H. Emulus – ARPT

6T is seen at Ballyconnell on 28th March 1959 taking on water prior to some shunting.

H. Emulus – ARPT

At Ballyconnell, Stationmaster Paddy O'Donnell, a native of Piltown, Kilkenny, stated that he had been in Ballyconnell only two years and he had only three predecessors since the line was opened. The first Stationmaster was a Mr. Wells, who was succeeded by his son, Mr. R. H. Wells. The only other Stationmaster was the late Mr. Andy Keirans, well known in Cavan GAA circles. Stationmaster O'Donnell, married man with five children, was of the opinion that the business people of Ballyconnell did not mind the closing down of the railway as long as they were provided with a good road service in its place.

CBPR loco is seen near Belturbet on a Dromod service, note the corrugated cottage and the unusual crossing signal.

J. Philips

Story of a historic beginning:

Opinions are divided as to why the narrow gauge railway line was originally established. One line of thought holds to the theory that it was to link the Arigna coalfields with the broad gauge of the former Midland Great Western Railway from Dublin to Sligo which passed through Co. Leitrim, and the Cavan line which made an end to end connection with the G.N.R at Cavan town. Others maintain that the line was put down to facilitate business, particularly cattle trading in Leitrim and West Cavan towns. In any event a company was formed to construct a 3ft gauge light railway and was registered under the name of the "Cavan, Leitrim and Roscommon Light Railway and Tramway Co. Ltd.". The original proposal was for an approximately 58 miles of railway and tramway and to run the line beyond Arigna as far as the railway at Boyle, with a connection from Rooskey Lough on the Shannon to Dromod. The latter scheme was rejected by the Privy Council which spoiled the company's plans for connecting with the Shannon steamer service. The Arigna-Boyle line though apparently authorised was never made. In 1895 Roscommon was dropped from the company's title which was then changed to the Cavan and Leitrim Railway Company.

3T is seen on the tramway on 14th March 1959, note the lake in background.

Bluebell Railway Museum Archive

Prior to its registration the company had obtained a report from an engineer, who was of the opinion that it would be impossible to lay a broad gauge line because of the number of peat bogs and lakes in the area through which it was proposed to run the line. Work on the laying of the line and erection of the workshops commenced in 1884. The contractors were Messrs. Collen Bros., Portadown. Some difficulty was experienced in construction near Tomkin Road where an embankment had to be put up to carry the line across the portion of a lake. Sometime after the lines were laid a section of the embankment slid into the lake and a diversion had to be made. There was also difficulty in getting firm foundations for bridges and culverts, and in one instance a foundation had to go down over 30ft in a bog. There was also trouble in the Ballinamore area where there was an objection to the building of the line across the Fair Green.

Despite all the obstacles, however, the work proceeded rapidly and soon the line was winding its way along the shores of lakes and rivers, through hill and bog. There were many sharp curves and gradients, naturally, but in all the circumstances a sound job was accomplished.

One Serious Accident:
One serious accident occurred during the work of construction. One March 15 1887, a contractor's train returning to Mohill collided with a donkey car near the Clooncahir crossing. All the wagons were derailed, three of the workers being killed, and a number injured. Eight locomotives were ordered from Messrs. Robert Stephenson and Co. Newcastle-on-Tyne, and each was given a name as follows; No 1 "Isabel", No 2 "Kathleen", No 3 "Lady Edith", No 4 "Violet", No 5 "Gertrude", No 6 "May", No 7 "Olive", No 8 "Queen Victoria." Subsequently another engine, "King Edward", was built for the company by the Stephenson firm. During most of its life "King Edward" worked bunker foremost as the rigidly coupled wheelbase was too hard on the track. It was withdrawn from service in 1934.

Lady Edith (Number 3) is seen at Ballinamore on 17th May 1924, note the original livery and nameplates .

K. Nunn; C&L Archive

The names given to the engines are thought to have been derived mostly from the Christian names of the wives and daughters of the first directors of the railway. What was known as the main line from Dromod to Belturbet, a distance of 33½ miles, connecting the Midland Great Western with the G.N.R., was opened for goods on October 18th 1887. A week later it was opened for passenger service. This stretch of line served Mohill, Ballinamore, Ballyconnell, as well as intermediate villages.

The Tramway Track:
The line from Ballinamore to Arigna, a distance of 14 ¾ miles, was opened on May 2nd 1888. This was known as the Tramway Track, having been laid along the public road from Ballinamore to Drumshanbo. The Roscommon Grand Jury had withdrawn their support for the remainder of the tramway from Arigna to Boyle, and as already indicated the branch from Ballinamore succeeded only in reaching Arigna, ending at a spot some distance from the village and the coal mines. All coal had to be carried approximately three miles to the railway.

3T is seen on the tramway Arigna bound on 14th March 1959.

4L is seen here on the tramway Ballinamore bound on 27th June 1957.

Some time after the opening, the bridge across the river Shannon gave some trouble. As a result, the engines, on account of their weight, were not allowed over it, and for a short period the wagons were drawn by horses from the bridge to Arigna.

The Shannon Bridge is seen from a carriage balcony.

John Wiltshire courtesy P. Brabham

The Shannon Bridge with 3T bound for Arigna on 14th March 1959.

Bluebell Railway Museum Archive

It is of interest to relate that although the line was not opened until October 17, 1887, goods traffic has been carried before that. On September 6 all the available wagons were used on a special train carrying pigs from Ballinamore fair to Dromod. Pig specials were also run to Belturbet and Dromod from the Mohill fair on October 5, 1887.

The Board of Trade regulations for the running of the train on the tramway between Ballinamore and Arigna were very stringent, and for sometime after it opened, the engines ran bogie first, duplicate driving gear being provided so that the driver could stand from the front. No protection from the weather was provided for the driver, who must have had a most unpleasant time. This regulation was later relaxed.

On the same murky day 3T is seen backing into its single carriage train at Arigna, the weather characterises the reality of the end.

*Bluebell Railway
Museum Archive*

Large Cow Catchers:

The original locomotives had stove pipe chimneys and large fireboxes to burn the local coal. Large cow catchers were on the front bufferbeam, and the wheels and motion of the engines used on the tramway were completely enclosed. In addition to the general 25mph speed limit over the whole Dromod – Belturbet section, the regulations specified 10 mph limits through all the passing places, 12 mph over the roadside section of the tramway, 4 mph over the oblique road crossings, with a compulsory stop immediately before: A figure of approximately £77,000 is given as the total loss to the ratepayers in the first twenty years of the railways existence, and the company struggled to keep going.

Many of the blind crossings on the branch had no gates like so many Irish tramways, the quintessential level crossing warning sign appeared at these spots.
Armstrong - ARPT

The Board of the Company consisted originally of five shareholders and six ratepayers' Directors. When the right of appointing baronial directors was transferred from the Grand Juries to the Co. Councils in 1898, the number of Directors representing Shareholders was increased to eight. At one stage an ambitious scheme was put forward to make the Cavan and Leitrim railway part of a coast to coast narrow gauge main line. The proposal was to connect up as a mixed gauge line from Greenore to Newry and then over the Bessbrook and Newry Tramway. A new line from Bessbrook was to provide a link with the Clogher Valley at Tynan, then onto Maguiresbridge. From the latter point it was proposed to lay a line to join the Cavan and Leitrim at Bawnboy Road. Eventually a connection would have been made to Roscommon, Tuam and Clifden. The new system was to have been called the Ulster and Connaught Light Railway, and a tunnel was actually built at Keady, County Armagh, to facilitate the project. However, the scheme fell through.

Dundalk, Newry and Geenore Railway loco Number 3, is seen approaching Greenore from Newry on a goods working on 29 Sep 1951, it was along here a dual gauge section of line was proposed.

Bluebell Railway Museum Archive

Met with Opposition:

The extension of the line to the Arigna mines met with opposition, and it was not until 1918 that a start was made under the Defence of the Realm Act. The extension was opened on June 2, 1920. During the last war coal supplies from England were cut off and the Arigna coal was used throughout Ireland. This brought improved business to the Cavan and Leitrim line, over which coal specials were an everyday occurrence.

All down the years the problem of replacement for the railway was a severe headache for the company. These came chiefly from the other narrow gauge systems such as the Cork, Blackrock and Passage Railway; the Tralee and Dingle Railways; Cork and Muskerry Railway, and the Clogher Valley Railway when it closed down. To the "man in the street" the most glamorous section of the Cavan and Leitrim is the Arigna Tramway – the branch line from Ballinamore. It is reputed to be the last remaining steam tramway in Ireland to maintain a passenger service.

4L seen at work on the tramway, with a train of coal wagons from Arigna on 27th June 1957.

Bluebell Railway Museum Archive

That in brief is a history of a famous railway line that is doomed to die on Tuesday next. Soon it will be no more, and with it will go the sturdy little engines that gave so much pleasure while "chug-chugging" their way through 72 years of Leitrim's storied history. And down memories lanes on Tuesday will go the sentimental to dwell again in an era when the Cavan and Leitrim was the pride and the joy of a hard-working people.

Alternative Road Service:

The following statement was issued on January 14th last by the general manager of C.I.E, Mr Frank Lemass: "The Board of C.I.E have announced with regret the decision to withdraw all passenger and freight train services from the Cavan and Leitrim section from the 1st April 1959, and consider that users of the services should be fully informed as to the reasons which compel this step, and of the alternative road services which will be provided for passengers and merchandise. Under the Transport Act 1958, C.I.E is obliged within a period of 5 years to be financially self-supporting and, to this end, it must effect radical economies. An obvious economy is to abandon services which are unremunerative and which show no possibility of being made remunerative.

Unfortunately, the Cavan and Leitrim section is in this category. It is a narrow gauge line which involves the physical transfer of all goods passing to and from the section, and the annual losses for many years have been substantial. For the year ended 31st March 1958, the loss, that is the excess of expenditure over revenue from the provisions of rail services on the section, was £40,000, and the estimated annual saving from which will accrue to the Board from the withdrawal of rail services, and after providing for the cost of substitute road services, is £32,000. The introduction of diesel traction on the section was previously considered and a careful re-examination has now been made to determine if having regard to the potential traffic on the section, there would be a reasonable prospect that that provision of diesel traction would make the section self-supporting. The examination revealed, however, that losses would still be incurred at an estimated annual rate of £33,000. The capital cost of diesel units and new passenger and goods vehicles, which would be required if the rail services were to be continued, would be £237,000.

CLOSING OF CAVAN AND LEITRIM RAILWAY

On and from Wednesday, 1st April, substitute bus services will be provided between Dromod and Ballinamore on weekdays, between Dromod and Belturbet on Mondays, Wednesdays and Fridays, and between Dromod and Arigna on Tuesdays, Thursdays and Saturdays as under:—

DROMOD — BALLINAMORE — BELTURBET — ARIGNA

WEEK-DAYS

		A.	B.	
		p.m.	p.m.	p.m.
Dromod	dept.	12.15	12.15	8.40
Mohill	,,	12.33	12.33	8.58
Fenagh	,,	12.53	12.53	9.18
Ballinamore	,,	1.2	1.2	9.25
Garadice Cross	,,	1.9	—	—
Ballyconnell	,,	1.33	—	—
Ballyduff	,,	—	1.10	—
Carnahone	,,	—	1.14	—
Annadale Cross	,,	—	1.21	—
Kiltubrid	,,	—	1.24	—
Greagh Cross	,,	—	1.28	—
Drumshanbo	,,	—	1.35	—
Arigna	,,	—	1.48	—
Mt. Allen Cross				
Belturbet	arr.	1.52	—	—

A — Mondays, Wednesdays and Friday, only.

		B.		A.	
		a.m.	p.m.	p.m.	p.m.
Belturbet	Dept.	—	—	4.20	—
Arigna	,,	—	4.15	—	—
Mt. Allen Cross					
Drumshanbo	,,	—	4.29	—	—
Greagh Cross	,,	—	4.35	—	—
Kiltubrid	,,	—	4.39	—	—
Annadale Cross	,,	—	4.42	—	—
Carnahone	,,	—	4.49	—	—
Ballyduff	,,	—	4.53	—	—
Ballyconnell	,,	—	—	4.41	—
Garadice Cross	,,	—	—	5.3	—
Ballinamore	,,	8.30	5.0	5.10	7.30
Fenagh	,,	8.38	—	—	7.38
Mohill	,,	9.0	—	—	8.0
Dromod	arr.	9.15	—	—	8.15

B—Tuesdays, Thursdays and Saturdays only.

Further particulars may be obtained on application to Road Passenger Manager, Amiens Street, Dublin, or to any of the Board's local Offices or Conductors.

CORAS IOMPAIR EIREANN

Alternative road service as advertised in the Anglo Celt.

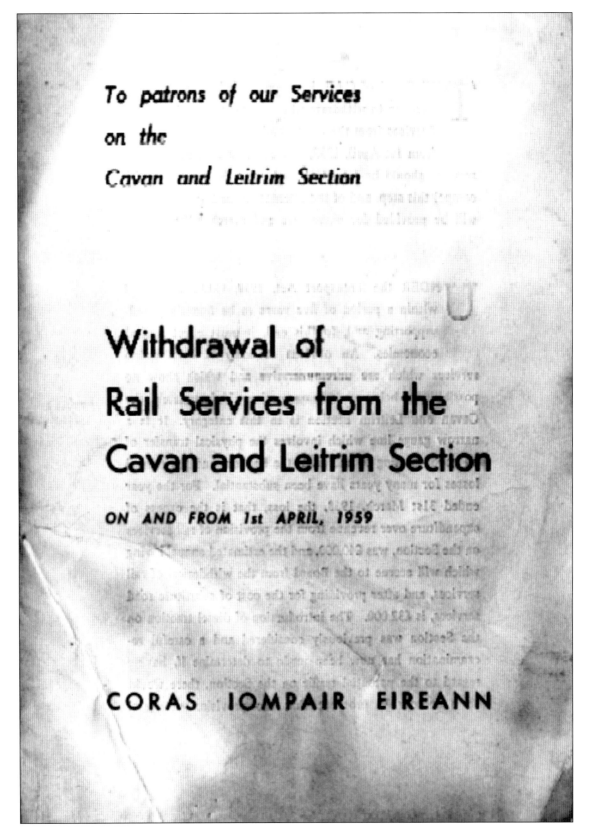

To patrons of our Services

on the

Cavan and Leitrim Section

Withdrawal of

Rail Services from the

Cavan and Leitrim Section

ON AND FROM 1st APRIL, 1959

CORAS IOMPAIR EIREANN

Closure pamphlet as issued by C.I.E.

C&L Archives

The Board intends to provide adequate alternative road services for both passengers and merchandise, as follows:- passengers: Bus services will be provided to connect with trains at Dromod. Two services will be operated on alternate weekdays between Ballinamore and Arigna and between Ballinamore and Belturbet. The principal places on the Arigna and Belturbet lines are served each weekday by the following bus services:- Arigna line 8:45am bus to Cavan to Sligo; 5.00pm bus Sligo to Cavan. Drumshanbo is also served by the Carrick-on-Shannon – Bundoran and Carrick-on-Shannon-Sligo bus services. Belturbet line – 2.20pm bus on weekdays and an additional bus at 6.40pm on Saturdays, Cavan to Enniskillen. 9.20 am bus on

weekdays and an additional bus at 5.25pm on Saturdays, Enniskillen to Cavan.

Services will be provided to convey merchandise, coal and livestock to and from railheads on the main line, and for regular supporters of the services the Board will continue to operate through rates with stations beyond railheads, based on the existing station to station rates. The Ballyhaise to Belturbet railway, one which merchandise trains only are operated, and which serves as a connecting line between the Cavan and Leitrim section and the Cavan – Dundalk section will be closed concurrently with the Cavan and Leitrim section, and the substitute road freight services will be extended to serve the area.

THE FINAL DAY

Then the final day of services came on Tuesday 31st March 1959, again this received much publicity and attracted huge crowds, both locals and enthusiasts. The following material gives a taster of what was experienced on that day, it is truly remarkable to look back and imagine what they witnessed and experienced. It could be argued that the Tralee and Dingle had overrun the Cavan and Leitrim as the majority of services and last trains were performed by T&D locos, with the 2-6-2T 5T hauling the last train to and from Arigna, 2-6-0T 6T hauling the last train to Belturbet, and the magnificent spectacle of a T&D double header with Kerr Stuart built 2-6-0T 4T and Hunslet 5T hauling the last train to and from Dromod.

Irish Rail Fans (Volume 5, 1959 No 2) recorded the last day in detail; Tuesday 31st March 1959 will be long revered in railway enthusiast circles as the last day of regular operation on the narrow-gauge Cavan & Leitrim system. The period leading up to the closure was one of great excitement. On Monday March 30 the IRRS (Irish Railway Record Society) organised a large party from Dublin and accordingly on the 08:00 from Ballinamore Loco 6T worked four coaches and two vans to Dromod for the return 12:20 service. One of these coaches was worked to Belturbet (Loco 6T) and two to Arigna (Loco 5T) while loco 4T with the fourth coach formed the 14:35 to Dromod. This loco had been in use in the morning on a special to Drumshanbo for clearance of goods wagons. All of these trains were very well filled and the Arigna train was escorted by half-a-dozen cars on the roadside sections but it was on the 19:00 Ballinamore-Dromod that the crowd was greatest.

While the image is of poor quality, it is important in that it shows 4T at the buffers at Dromod on the last day of services with the final 14:35 train to Dromod.

Leitrim Library

The train was two coaches and van hauled by 6T. On March 31 loco 6T also performed the "lion's share" of the work on the 08:00 to Dromod, 12:20 thence to Belturbet and 16:20 back to Ballinamore. Again crowds travelled on all trains, loco 5T worked two crammed coaches to Arigna and 6T also had two for Belturbet, but the 19:00 - the real climax of the day - was double-headed: Locos 5T and 4T with coach 7L, van 14L, coaches 5L, 6L, 21L, 1L and van 18L - the entire working stock. This monster train was well filled and many came to pay their last respects at crossings and halts en-route while the salute of detonators was at times ear-splitting. Speeches were made at Dromod and a meeting held after the train returned to Ballinamore to protest at the immediate lifting of the track which commenced on April 1. Strangely, the line is to be lifted outwards from Ballinamore to Belturbet and Dromod (the Arigna line will be dealt with by road) and the stock will be broken up, it is said, at these places.

It is anticipated that coaches 1L and 7L, some engines, and possibly loco 6T, will be transferred to the West Clare section. The 'substitute' service is provided by one bus. It works from Ballinamore to Dromod on weekdays at 08:30 and returns at 12:15 whence it continues to Belturbet and back on Mondays, Wednesdays and Fridays and serves Arigna on Tuesdays, Thursdays and Saturdays. It also runs to Dromod on weekdays at 19:30 and returns at 20:40. The freight side is being handled by lorry services based on Dromod, Carrick-on-Shannon and Cavan. From the foregoing it will be seen that Ballinamore suffers considerably from the closure - the railway was the largest employer in this small town - and is not even recompensed by the basing of road freight services there.

Here we see the wagon shop in February 1959, the workshop often turned out complete rebuilds of wagons, the Ballinamore men had fine skills on display.

National Library Ireland

Even as late as February 1959 the works still carried on with routine maintenance, here we see 8L in works with its driving wheels on show and pistons removed, it was undergoing an overhaul at the time, and was subsequently scrapped in situ.

National Library Ireland

P.B Whitehouse also gave an inspiring personal extract on the last trains to and from Dromod in his book "Narrow Gauge Album, 1966". We thank Michael Whitehouse for providing us with permission to publish the extract.

It was depressing to see the Cavan and Leitrim in its last years, its engines were generally filthy inside as well as out, and with the exception of 6T, which had been done up at Inchicore in 1957, were in poor condition.

6T seen at Dromod on 14th March 1959, with steam leaking everywhere.

Bluebell Railway Museum Archive

Its coaches were little better and in some case it was obvious their bodies had been crudely repaired just to keep the sides vertical – one rebodied with an assemblage of old bus parts. At the time of closure there were but five coaches serviceable, the converted bus No 7L, two open ended bogie coaches 5L and 6L, an ex Tralee and Dingle coach (in good condition) 21L and a rebuilt Cavan and Leitrim bogie coach 1L. There were, however, two saving graces- the condition of the track, which was excellent, and the spirit of the men.

1L seen at Ballinamore, this was the last flowering of Ballinamore works, note the enclosed balcony ends.

J. Powell

The last day of working was 31 March 1959, and it was 6T which bore the brunt of that day – she was the only engine in what could be termed reasonable condition. Service began with the 8 a. m Ballinamore to Dromod, where the Cavan and Leitrim connected with the old Midland Great Western Railway. Here it waited for the diesel from Dublin, eighty or so miles away, and this arrived punctually at 11:52 bringing with it the inevitable hoard of "last day" travelling enthusiasts. Among these were included visitors from as far afield as Glasgow and Hampshire, not forgetting a priest in a flowing cassock which proved little hindrance when it came to positioning for photography.

By then 6T had been turned and backed down to the head of four bogie coaches, each apparently older than the next. There were also two vans in case the overflow of passengers made these necessary. The four passenger coaches representing 80% of the section's serviceable vehicles, the other 20% standing in the siding nearby, consisted of the best of the lot, one being the Tralee and Dingle composite 21L. The crowd lost no time in looking for relics of the older days, and they were not hard to find for the wagons scattered about the sidings must have come from every narrow gauge line to come into the hands of the Great Southern Railway.

6T departs Dromod with the last 12:20 train, note the eclectic mix of rolling stock gathered.

IRRS

At 12:20 the driver got the "green" and the cloud of briquette smoke which had clothed the narrow-gauge bay became even worse as 6T moved off at brisk pace towards Mohill and Ballinamore where it arrived at 2pm, the time it was due away to Belturbet! After a shunt, and the acquisition of some vitally needed water, 6T was off again with two coaches and some wagons to Belturbet an hour late. Most of the passengers having opted for the Arigna branch train due out at 1:50pm. Belturbet platform was thronged with people, and to add to the confusion a wagon load of sheep was attached to the return train for dropping off at Ballyconnell. The 4.20pm train for Ballinamore left at 5.30pm to the accompaniment of the usual fog signals, finally reaching Ballinamore at 6.25pm. when the whole station and its environs were packed with humanity.

5T departs Ballinamore with the final working for Arigna.

IRRS

6T arrives at Ballinamore and will eventually carry on to Belturbet.

IRRS

Meanwhile 5T had set off for Arigna at 2.33pm complete with two open ended bogie coaches 5L and 6L (taken off the morning train from Dromod) plus five wagons. Even this late start was only managed by the staff rounding up the intending passengers who were widely scattered about Ballinamore yards poking round for items of interest. By dint of much whistling all assembled and the "Right Away", given by the genial sandy haired guard, whose instructions to the driver were "Stop everywhere, Paddy". Stops were made at all the hedge halts down the line for photographic purposes both by the passengers and the posse of motorists who were following the train. There was even a purple skirted lady who knelt in the road to obtain the required low angle shots. So flanked by outriders the train steamed into Drumshanbo where a tape recorder was playing Irish folk music and a vociferous local inhabitant distributed leaflets describing the attractions of the neighbourhood at the same time forecasting doom when the line closed. The wagons were dropped off here, it would have been impossible to shunt them with the two coaches so jammed with people.

5T on the tramway at Kiltubrid.

IRRS

5T is seen on the tramway at Annadale, 5T was rarely out of use since she was sent to the North West some 8 years previously.

IRRS

5T at Arigna being waved off, history was made.

Arigna was reached three-quarters of an hour late at 4pm and here 5T needed the protection of local Garda to reach the turntable and turn. In view of the late arrival the guard decided that the return would be 4:24pm and not 4:15 as advertised, and this welcome relief enabled 5T's driver to attend to the nuts on her piston gland which had been blowing all the way up despite attention during the "photographic stops". The train left, to shouts, cheers and detonations, and after fifteen minutes arrived at Drumshanbo where a local councillor harangued the crowd for five minutes or so, making repeated references to the days of independence (for local people the railway was work and they never took too kindly to the Great Southern or CIE).

C&L Archive

5T at Drumshanbo returning to Ballinamore.
Leitrim Observer

After some presentations the train got underway once more. At 5:15pm, it was now thirty-seven minutes late, which wasn't bad considering the wagons left behind on the outward journey had to be shunted and water taken as well. Once again stops were made at all the halts where the local people had turned out to cheer the train on its way, and a further half an hour was lost before reaching Ballinamore. The arrival almost coincide with that of the 4.50pm from Dromod which came in behind 4T complete with Tralee and Dingle composite and a motley collection of vans and wagons. The only Cavan and Leitrim engine in steam was 4L (formerly named "Violet") shunting in the yard.

Loco 4L is seen on shed in an awful condition, with 4T preparing to depart the shed to gather her train for Dromod, as seen previously.
Colour Rail

The last rites were to begin at 7pm with the departure of the final train to Dromod, and this eventually left at 7:38pm with the whole of the passenger stock still able to run. The train was double-headed by 4T and 5T and all the coaches were crammed to the end platforms with people. All the way along the line the locals turned out to pay their tribute and Dromod was reached just under an hour late to the accompaniment of the town band. The 6pm Dublin to Sligo railcar gave long blasts on its klaxon horn as did the 7:30pm Sligo – Dublin diesel-electric, and 4T and 5T replied with their whistles. Both engines were turned and eventually the 8:40pm left for Ballinamore just over an hour late accompanied by much noise and cheering and shouting. Despite heavy rain there were small crowds at all the halts and stations who had come to bid their own railway farewell. Ballinamore was reached at 11.08pm well over an hour and twenty minutes late, and here the whole town must have turned out. The coaches were left in the platform and the engines quietly moved off to the shed. The Drumshanbo councillor once again harangued the crowd until just before midnight, and then silence descended on the last day of service on the Cavan and Leitrim Railway.

The railway enthusiast perspective has been looked at, now we take a look at the local reaction. As can be expected this was a major event in local news stories and was well documented. The Anglo Celt continued its feature on the system, recording the last trains.

"Cavan and Leitrim comes to final halt" (April 1959)

Thousands Give it a Resounding Farewell

Cheers, Fog-Signals And A Tinge of Sorrow

In a blaze of glory, in keeping with its splendid tradition of 72 years' service, the Cavan and Leitrim Railway steamed into oblivion on Tuesday night after the last train had made a historic run from Dromod to the head-quarters of the system at Ballinamore. And what a farewell it was given; The hills of Leitrim resounded to the explosion of fog-signals and lusty cheers of the thousands who converged on all sections of the railway to give a hearty send-off to an old friend. From all parts of Leitrim and Cavan they came and from outside counties as well – the young and the old – all intent on being present at an epoch-making event, and the closing chapter in Leitrim's chequered history.

Joy mingled with sorrow at every phase of Tuesday nights "obsequies" – joy for the legions of happy boys and girls who sang and danced their way on the last trains from Drumshanbo, from Belturbet, from Dromod; sorrow for the stolid, weather-beaten rail men who had grown up with the "narrow-gauge" and who could vividly recall every milestone of its halcyon days.

Surely, too, as we sped northwards from Dromod through the rain laden night on that last 16 miles journey to Ballinamore, the ghosts of old Leitrim must have watched our passing, while the Valhalla of the railroads if such there be – prepared a fitting reception for the hero of the century. Two of the faithful old engines took the train on its last journey, and every available carriage was brought into service to accommodate the big crowd which pushed and jostled at every stop to gain a foothold, however precarious. Good humour prevailed everywhere and all discomforts were greeted with a smile.

6T readying to depart Dromod on 28th March 1959.
H Emulus - ARPI

5T on Arigna line penultimate day services, note the carriage balconies are crammed.

C&L Archives

A big ovation awaited the train at Dromod when it arrived to prepare for the return journey to Ballinamore. The passengers of whom there must easily have been 500 – filtered on to the platform in the misty rain to get a "breather" before commencing the last lap home. The dromod boys and girls flageolet band in charge of Mrs. Elizabeth Moffatt, played martial airs on the platform and carried placards with the words "There goes another Irish Railway"; "Farewell to the Narrow Gauge"; "You were taken from us and replaced by foreign power"; "We will miss your familiar whistle"; and "The end of the line". The band was playing "kitty from Ballinamore" as we scrambled aboard the train after a delay of about half an hour. The shrill shrieks of the engine whistles merged with the sounds of exploding fog signals as the train moved slowly out at 9:45pm. It was exactly one hour and five minutes behind time, but no one cared, because no one was in a hurry!

Just before the take off, the narrow gauge got a salute from the sleek, aristocratic Dublin to Sligo diesel which hooted its farewell from the broad gauge line as it slid speedily from the station on its journey westwards.

It was raining heavily now, but that did not deter the exuberant passengers from leaning crazily out of open windows and swinging dangerously from open doorways. Space was at a premium. What you had you held, and "let the devil take the hintermost". One was left wondering where all the little boys and girls came from, or how many of them would be missing at the end of the line. One unfortunate guy named "Tom Dooley" certainly had a most unpleasant time, he fell from that train at least a hundred times in the short journey. The crush was great, but the fun also was great, and time sped all too quickly in the care-free atmosphere.

What the last train must have looked like, here we see a double headed train with a CBPR and C&L loco at the helm.

Leitrim County Library

Rollicking Songs:

The repertoire of rollicking songs about Co. Leitrim must be never ending – or so it would seem from the grand selection we had from the group of Mohill girls. "Where the Shannon Waters flow" got a huge reception; so, too, did that song about "Selton Hill", and, of course "Sweet Mohill" was immensely popular. "If we only has the narrow gauge over here" crowned the efforts of this talented group. Then there was the jolly couple who cause much amusement by recounting how they missed the outward train at Mohill after sending their car ahead and had to hire a car to reach the next stop. The male of the party, with a pronounced American accent, got great fun out of the retelling of that story.

Dereen halt, so close to the train that it was nearly possible to touch the gatehouse by leaning out a window, brought us more fog signals, plus a few passengers who were somehow squeezed in. More songs, and in no time we were moving slowly into the crowded platform at Mohill to a deafening cacophony of hooting, whistling, explosions, cheers "Up Mohill" and counter cheers of "Up Ballinamore!"

Here we were sorry to part with our bevy of singing girls, but their place was quickly taken by others who entrained and soon the "house full" notice was up again. Mohill slid behind and soon we were again out in the darkness of the Leitrim countryside. The youngsters of the train had, if anything, become more daring and the Zooligocal Gardens on its busiest day would have been a picnic compared to the strenuous efforts of retaining equilibrium in the confined spaces of these narrow gauge carriages.

Survival of the Fittest:

Adoon, Fenagh, Lauderdale, slipped by, and the excitement mounted as we approached the end of the line. The distant signals of Ballinamore was the signal for a concerted rush to all vantage points. It was now certainly a question of the survival of the fittest. The sandwiches provided a la carte in Dromod stood us in good stead, and we held our own.

The hooting of our engines, it seemed took on a defiant, exultant note, as we entered the brightness of the terminus, to the accompaniment of tumultuous cheers from the awaiting throng, the incessant explosion of fog signals, and the constant flash of camera bulbs.

Here we see gate mistress Molly Derwin at Clooncolry gates on the last day 31st March 1959, this road marks the present day limit of the preserved C&L.

C&L Archives

We moved forward slowly through the milling crowd and came to a reluctant, hissing stop. The end of the line has been reached and the days of the Cavan and Leitrim Railway were over. The time was 11:10pm – one hour 25 minutes after leaving Dromod, only twenty minutes over the time allowed in normal circumstances for the journey. The "narrow gauge" had lived up to its reputation of good timing even in its dying moments.

Ballinamore platforms are packed following the return of the double headed special.
Leitrim County Library

A second view of the crowded platforms at Ballinamore.

Ballinamore shed seen on 28th March 1959, the air of decay is self evident.

There were animated scenes at the station as the passengers poured out on the platform. There were handshakes all round, and the drivers, firemen, and guards received many congratulatory messages and good wishes for the future. Many went to the front of the train to have a last look at the engines, which still pulsated with life as if eager to be off on another run.

Not an Unseemly Incident:

The orderly scenes came as an anti-climax to those who had forecast the "tearing asunder" of the train by souvenir hunters when the last run was over. Souvenir hunters were there, but they went about their business unobtrusively in an orderly manner, collecting mementoes of an historic occasion.

There was not one incident to mar the great occasion, which is to the undying credit of the thousands who took part in the last performance of a famous railway. The crews of the last train were; Driver Bennie McGuinness; a native of Co. Louth, and fireman Francis Kelly, a native of Tuam; driver William McManus, a native of Athlone, and Fireman J. J. Callery of Leitrim Hill. The guard was William Burns of Ballinamore, assisted by Paddy Halligan of Cavan and Tommy Eagan of Athlone.

Drumshanbo Send-off:

Earlier in the evening the last train from Ballinamore, Mohill and Dromod left Drumshanbo to the strains of "Auld Lang Syne", sung by a large crowd on the platform. (Fog signals exploded, and the whistle of the train blew continuously). Present on the platform was 93 years old P. Kelly of Congress Terrace, Drumshanbo, who was at the erection of the bridge spanning the railway outside the town and the turntable for engines at Arigna. Mr. J. M. Mooney, Co. C.. whose father was one of the directors of the railway, wished the train Godspeed and farewell on its journey.

Arigna turntable with 2L being turned.

John Wiltshire courtesy Peter Brabham

Here we see the crowded platforms of Drumshanbo on the last day..

Leitrim Observer

The last goods from Drumshanbo fell to Kerr Stuart 4T.

Leitrim County Library

Belturbet Excitement:
There were exciting scenes at Belturbet as the last train let for Ballinamore at 5:30pm. It was due to leave at 4:20pm but was delayed by the hundreds of railway enthusiasts who surrounded the platform. Souvenir hunters picked up everything that had any connection with the railway – labels, bolts, tickets, signs, etc. Coins were laid on the lines to have them flattened by the wheels of the train.

A wagon of sheep was dispatched from Belturbet for Mr. Joseph Baxter, victualler, Ballyconnell – the last livestock to be carried on the line. Incidentally, Mr. Baxter's late father, was one of the first to transport livestock when the line opened 72 years ago. As the train left the station to the accompaniment of exploding fog signals and ringing cheers, passengers were clinging on to every vantage point. Carriages were so full that some passengers were carried in livestock wagons. Some of those who could not find accommodation on the train made the journey by car to Ballyconnell and there boarded the train for Ballinamore.

Missed train at Ballyconnell:
At Ballyconnell the scenes of animation were repeated. Mr Owe Reilly, Ballinamore, a returned railway official, who was making the journey from Belturbet to Ballinamore, disembarked at Ballyconnell to view the T.V. film of the narrow gauge in a local house. On his return journey he was dismayed to find that the train had pulled out in his absence and he had missed the last run home.

All along the line from Ballyconnell to Ballinamore people left their houses to wave a last farewell to the passing train, and there were enthusiastic scenes when it reached Ballinamore at 6:50pm.

The Alternative Service:
Officials of the CIE visited the various centres throughout the area to superintend the change over to road passenger and freight service, which came into operation on Wednesday morning. It was emphasised by local officials that improved and more flexible services would now operate to and from all areas previously served by the narrow gauge, and also outlying areas. The officials at Ballinamore on Tuesday night included Messrs M. Dowling, chief Inspector, Road passenger section; J. Keenan, Assistant Road traffic manager; M. Culligan, research assistant traffic department; W. Boyle, chief superintendent.

Mopping up operations:
It is understood that most of the railway staff will remain in the area to take part in the "mopping up" operations which will take some months to complete. It is intended to transfer most of the rolling stock to the West Clare narrow gauge railway. On Wednesday permanent way workmen commenced lifting all the sidings at Ballyconnell station. It is rumoured that the Belfast Museum is negotiating the purchase of one of the old engines and a coach to preserve for future generations.

LIFTING OF THE LINE

The lifting then began in earnest, and the Cavan and Leitrim was no more. The lifting was undertaken in sections starting from Ballinamore and working out along the main line in both directions towards Dromod and Belturbet. Meanwhile the Arigna branch was lifted by road. Irish Rail Fans (Volume 5, 1959, Number 5) reported that, Considerable progress has already been made and in late May the Arigna line had been lifted between Ballinamore (Main Street Gates) and MP 3½, on a few short isolated stretches thence to Creagh, and between Creagh and Arigna Station (except for the non-roadside stretch into Drumshanbo and the yard there). At Mahanagh Bridge, where the line crossed the Shannon, a 100 yard length has been left in situ to aid removal of the girders while the entire Derreenavoggy extension remains intact. On the Dromod - Ballinamore main line only the sidings at Mohill and a siding in Dromod have been lifted but between Ballinamore and Belturbet the track is being removed working out from Ballinamore. At the time of writing, some 2½ miles have been removed and as the lifting is being done by rail, locos 3T, 4T and 10L have been isolated beyond the rail break. The locomotives stable overnight in Ballyconnell; one is in use for the lifting train, one on material removal trains and the third spare. The lifting train includes six ex CB&PR open wagons, bereft of sides, in use as rail wagons.

The Tramway section at Gallery Road being lifted.

6T at Dromod with van 17L, in the summer of 1959.

C&L Archive

Locomotive 8L has been cut up and the remains removed from Ballinamore. It is expected that the three locomotives isolated in the Belturbet section will be cut up at Belturbet when the lifting is complete. Loco 3L - formerly named "Lady Edith" - and the ex Tralee & Dingle coach 21L have been purchased by an American for preservation in working order near New York. Accordingly these two vehicles were despatched from Dublin by boat consigned to "The Lady Edith Society". Coaches 1L and 7L together with a variety of wagons are in Dromod marked "for West Clare" but there is now no indication of the transfer of a locomotive to that section. Coaches 5L and 6L have been sold to a local sports association but the remainder of the locos and rolling stock are in Ballinamore where demolition of wagons is proceeding.

6T with the lifting train at Ballinamore on 25th August 1959.

R. Joanes

The goods loop siding at Dromod had been lifted.

National Library Ireland

Ballinamore platform with the remains of rolling stock scattered along the platform.

R Joanes

A unique image of 3L on a broad gauge wagon in what looks to be the Dublin area, she was a fortunate survivor and emigrated like so many Irish men and women to America, Imagine if she returned to her C&L home?

Colour Rail

In a scene that reflects the last train we see a T&D double header with 6T and 4T, 4T had failed with a lifting train at Adoon and 6T was sent to the rescue.

National Library Ireland

The next edition of Irish Rail Fans (Volume 6, 1959, Number 4) reported on the further progress of lifting, The branch from Ballinamore station to Arigna station is now lifted completely but the extension thence to Derreenavoggy is still intact and no effort has been made to remove it. The bridge over the Shannon at Mahanagh has not been dismantled as expected but it is fenced off at each end and the track to it removed. Almost all the track from the Arigna line has been purchased by Comlucht Siúicre Éireann *(Irish Sugar Company)* for use on their lines under construction on Gowla Bog. A few of the best sections have, however, been sent to the West Clare for renewals there.

This image while not the best quality is significant in that it shows a lifting train in colour with 10L on the Belturbet section.

C&L Archive

On the Ballinamore - Belturbet line work is complete to within two miles of Belturbet. Of the locos isolated on the section, 3T has been cut up but 4T and 10L remain at work. Rails and sleepers are still being loaded into standard gauge wagons at Belturbet but when work on the narrow gauge is completed the four mile branch of the former GNR thence to Ballyhaise will be removed. On Thursday September 3 the Ballinamore - Dromod lifting train commenced operations by breaking the track at Ballinamore and is now working towards Dromod.

2L and 4L stabled at Mohill.

C&L Archive

Belturbet station with C&L rails awaiting collection note a former broad gauge Great Southern and Western Railway J15 0-6-0 in the background.

R Joanes

Three locomotives (2L, 4L and 6T) are thus stabled at Mohill although the last mentioned is likely to bear the brunt of the work. Loco 12L is disabled at Dromod close to coach 7L which, contrary to expectations, does not seem to be destined for West Clare as its seats have been removed and it is in a poor state of repair both internally and externally. Coach 1L has already been transferred to that section as mentioned elsewhere in this issue. At Ballinamore coach 6L, 8 open wagons and four cattle wagons have been isolated, while coach 5L and van 16L have been moved to Mohill with other wagons in use on the lifting trains.

Devastation at Dromod, all items of the permanent way were brought here to be used elsewhere. Note the sleepers, farm gates complete with trespass signs, rails, crossing gates. Also see one engine has been scrapped, likely to be 4L, a carriage remains at the end of the former coal siding. Note the former mainline, all ripped up as far as the station throat.

National Library Ireland

Also seen at the coal sidings at Dromod, 2L is stabled over a culvert, note the gradient posts and baseplates beside her. This culvert can be viewed from C&L trains today.

Irish Rail Fans provide a final update (Volume 6, 1960, Number 1), with the exception of approximately 3 miles of the Ballinamore - Dromod section from Dromod to a point beyond Dereen Halt, and the 1½ mile long extension from Arigna Station to Derreenavoggy Collieries, the entire trackwork of the 3' gauge Cavan & Leitrim system has now been removed. In addition to those mentioned in our last issue, loco 12L is at present being cut up in Dromod and when lifting of the remaining short stretch of track is completed the three surviving locos - 2L, 4L and 3T - are likely to be scrapped as well.

2L "Kathleen" and former composite 5L lay abandoned at Dromod for sometime after lifting, here they are seen in 1960. They were restored to their C&L condition and can now be viewed in Cultra.

David Waldren Collection

Lifting of the Ballinamore - Belturbet section was completed in October and the two locos (4T and 10L) isolated in Belturbet were cut up there. In addition to loco 3L and coach 21L, loco 5T was bought by, the "Lady Edith Society" and all three are now preserved in "Pleasure Island", Wakefield, Massachusetts. Coaches 5L, 7L and van 16L are in Dromod and are the only coaching vehicles remaining.

12L awaiting its fate at Dromod, preservationists discovered a cab porthole which could be from this loco.

R Joanes

And so the last remnants of the C&L vanished. However, it was to be remembered locally in the legends of time. Buildings survived at most of the principle stations along the route, Dromod yard was cleared by CIE and became a stabling area for school buses, the engine shed was engulfed with ivy. The station building survived, however it hadn't been in use since 1925 when the Great Southern moved ticket sales to the broad gauge station. Ballinamore became a shadow of its former self but became part of the local school and retains the stonework of the engine shed, and the fine brick building survives. Belturbet never had a C&L station to speak of, however the Great Northern building and train shed became a ruin with cattle roaming among the yard. The station building at Arigna still stands but the alignment was covered by the road.

Some of the wagons and carriages were sold locally, 6L becoming the changing room of the local GAA club at Ballinamore. The Cavan and Leitrim Railway (Dromod) recovered the original balcony cast iron ends from the remains of the carriage. We also recovered parts from a brake van 17L, these remain in store for a possible replication, and the balcony was incorporated into our new build balcony coach 13L.

Some of the stock (as referred to in the text) was also transferred to the West Clare section, including carriage 1L and a number of wagons to live out the next year on the Atlantic coast. Bord na Mona (Irish Turf Board) purchased 1L and a number of West Clare wagons when that line closed in 1961. 1L became a grounded coach body on the Bellacorrick system. Unfortunately, it was burnt by accident in the late 80's. This coach represented the end of the C&L craftsmanship, it is unfortunate it doesn't survive.

Of the locomotives two original Cavan and Leitrim 4-4-0T locos survive with 2L "Kathleen" preserved in Cultra, Co. Down in company of original Cavan and Leitrim composite 5L. Loco 3L "Lady Edith" is preserved in New Jersey at the Pine Creek Railroad, while there have been rumours of her return nothing concrete has materialised. We at the Cavan and Leitrim (Dromod) would very much love to see Lady Edith on home ground at Dromod. We would encourage people who may like to help to contact us. Lady Edith also is in the company of two Tralee and Dingle carriages (of much interest to the writer!) they are a former brake 3rd 2T of 1890, and composite 18T of 1907) and a CIE built luggage trailer mounted on a Clogher Valley chassis.

While not a Cavan and Leitrim loco, former Tralee and Dingle Light Railway 2-6-2T 5T also went to America and came back, having been separated from Lady Edith. 5T was restored to steam on the line at Blennerville and is not likely to run anytime soon, having not run in over 10 years. We at Dromod would also welcome 5T's return to the North West, 5T did haul the last trains and we hope to have an original T&D carriage in service.

1L seen on the Bellacorrick system in June 1973.

Philip Bedford Collection, original photographer unknown

REVITALIZATION OF THE C&L

The stories and legend of the C&L were to inspire its recreation. An unofficial group known as the Irish Narrow Gauge Trust (INGT) had set up a small museum in Cahir, Co. Tipperary and had started to collect 2 and 3ft gauge locos and rolling stock. Unfortunately promised grant aid did not materialise and like so many other preservation schemes, the group looked elsewhere. The INGT looked at some former broad gauge stations in Connemara but these were deemed unsuitable for various reasons. They then made a visit to Dromod on 9th August 1992. It was this trip that led to the revival and re-formation of the Cavan and Leitrim Railway.

The original GSR era Dromod bilingual sign now preserved at the station.

C&L

Site pre preservation in the late 80's.

C&L Archive

Shed covered in ivy upon inspection on that August day.

C&L

They called to Dromod more in hope, they were surprised to find that the site was largely intact save for the narrow gauge goods shed which had been demolished. The engine shed and water tower were intact albeit engulfed in a sea of ivy. They fought through ivy and entered the former engine shed, the smell of soot still hung in the air as though the locos were still there. The former narrow gauge yard was full of clutter and weeds, however after fighting on along the old alignment and rubbish it became clear that the trackbed was intact ¾ mile towards Ballinamore. This section went as far as Clooncolry where the first level crossing was located.

On returning from the inspection, they examined the former narrow gauge station which was in a good condition, and on enquiring found that it had been empty for a number of years. The owners Oliver and Mary Shanley were asked if the former station could be bought and if they would like a narrow gauge railway in their garden, they answered without hesitation yes! The move from Cahir began on 22nd December 1992 and was completed on 22 January 1993. More than forty lorry loads of equipment had to be moved, some of it involving cranes at Cahir and Dromod. The weather deteriorated in January and they had to contend with snow, ice, torrential rain and gale force winds.

Shed clearance underway in 1993, a tracked machine was brought in to remove the bushes.

C&L Archive

Track laying has commenced in 1993 using ex West Clare track acquired from Bord na Mona, in this image rail access has returned to the engine shed, the carriage shed has been created. Note the NCC wagon 4318 in the foreground .

C&L Archive

Temporary 3ft gauge track was laid through Shanley's garden to accommodate much of the rolling stock already gathered. Work then began clearing the yard in June 1993, trees and bushes were cut down and burnt, the shed was reclaimed from the ivy. After a lot of manual labour, a large tracked machine was hired to finish clearing and levelling the site. The machine spent 8 days digging out drains, uncovered old cars, and clearing off the first mile of trackbed. The engine shed rood was also completely renewed.

Funding from the EU and the International Fund for Ireland totalling £143,000 helped the reinstatement of the carriage shed, the construction of a new 4 road workshop as well as relaying some of the ½ mile of the original line. The Cavan and Leitrim Railway Supporters Association was also set up as the fundraising arm of the railway while the Cavan and Leitrim Railway Ltd. was established to hold the legal and insurance responsibilities etc.

May 1994 saw track laying commence within the station yard. Rail was recovered from the Littelton area of Bord na Mona, this is mostly former West Clare 60lb rail and was sufficient for the first section of track.

Motive Power and rolling stock:

The Cavan and Leitrim Railway is the proud custodian of two Bristol Wagon and Carriage Company built Tralee and Dingle Light Railway 3rd class carriages in original condition, numbers 7T and 10T, built in 1890 and 1891 respectively. 10T remains in as recovered condition and is intact, stepping into this vehicle is like stepping back in time to a bygone age. 7T's body was rotten, however the chassis is in good order and original TDLR bogies have been recovered from 48C (8T).

TDLR 10T on site in 1993, 10T was built by Bristol in 1891 so just over 100 years old when this image was taken. Note the chassis of 7T to the right with original bench.

C&L Archive

In the spirit of the former line, the new preserved line has rolling stock and motive power from other railways also more Munster invaders! This included the ex West Clare section CIE railcar trailer 47c, and the remains of 48c. 47c despite being recovered in a derelict condition was made ready for the first services in May 1995. Some jewels of the narrow gauge collection included several ex West Clare section GSR built goods vans, and a unique survivor in the form of an LMS NCC narrow gauge 2 plank wagon, intact and fully restored at Dromod. An interesting fact is that BNCR wagons and a loco were sent to Ballinamore when the railway was under government control, it's very possible the wagon was one of those brought down.

Steam motive power was naturally vital for such an organisation, the group had since 1988 been restoring a Kerr Stuart built 0-4-2T at Alan Kcof Ltd. This was works number 3024, built in 1916 and was formerly named "Sir Murray Morrison", it was a contractor's engine and was bought by British Aluminium for use on the Lochaber railway. When we recovered it, all that remained was the chassis, wheels, cylinders and chimney, everything else was gone. The group commissioned Keef Ltd. to rebuild the loco, this has included a boiler, new tanks and a cab, the back of which has been styled like a T&D cab, cowcatchers

were also fitted, and she was renamed more appropriately as "Dromad". She arrived at Dromod on 11th July 1994 and steamed successfully 2 days after, and was the first steam loco since 6T hauled the last lifting train to steam on site.

Our Avonside built steam loco "Nancy" has been our most ambitious restoration project. She was built in Bristol in 1908 works number 1547. Her restoration was widely reported in both the local and enthusiast media. This loco had a long restoration over 22 years costing £160,000 and returned to her new home in 2019. She has since returned steam to the C&L after a drought of some years, when Dromad's ticket expired.

60th commemorations:
Nancy's arrival:
Nancy arrived on an auspicious weekend, the 60th anniversary of closure of the Cavan and Leitrim railway. She arrived on 30th March and was on C&L metals the next day and also steamed successfully, the very day services ended 60 years previously. This was by far the best commemoration we could give. To think we were steaming along the same alignment, from the same platform like those services throughout the years.

Nancy at platform with dome, compare this with H. Emulus' view of Dromod with 6T.

C&L Archive

Nancy seen at Dromod engine shed, this is a unique feature in that it is the oldest engine shed in daily service to this day, having been constructed in 1887, it continues to shed an active steam locomotive and is no display!

Colm Mulligan

Ballinamore and Drumshanbo:

No sooner had Nancy arrived at Dromod and she was off on further travels to parts of the former C&L network, that have been without steam since 1959. Ballinamore was visited first on 2nd June 2019, this was in conjunction with the South Leitrim West Cavan Vintage Club, Nancy being the star attraction at the Ballinamore Family Day. Both myself and Micheal stayed overnight like so many C&L enginemen did throughout the years at Ballinamore station. I had the privilege of lighting the fire in Nancy the following morning, almost 60 years after the last fire was lit. The day was very enjoyable with many locals coming down and giving their stories of the line and how they remembered it.

Nancy steaming down Main Street in Drumshanbo, with Nigel Billett on the footplate.

Gerry Faughnan

Next Nancy headed down the Arigna branch towards Drumshanbo, to take part in the An Tóstal festival. Nancy was steamed on the move, with myself at the controls. A photo stop was made on the site of the original station beside the old water tower, before steaming through the town (literally) whistling down the main street of Drumshanbo. Who knows where Nancy will go next!

Industrial Collection:

The railway also holds several industrial locos and rolling stock from Irish railways. This includes Irish Turf Board's railcar C11 and diesel loco LM11, both built in Germany by Sollinger & Hutte and Ruhrtahler respectively, they were built during the 1930's due to the economic war with the UK at the time. These two locos became Bord na Mona's first railcar and diesel loco. The collection has since grown to include varieties of Ruston, Simplex, Deutz, Gleismac locomotives, all of which worked with Bord na Mona throughout the years. The railway has also built a 3ft gauge inspection bicycle from scratch (based on a C&L prototype) using original Teetor and Hartley wheels, which was graced by none other than Michael Portillo! Michael came to Dromod as part of the BBC production "Great Railway Journeys". Along with a new build pump trolley (based on a Bord na Mona design of 1945) and is unique to Ireland. Some other notable examples include a tipper wagon from the construction of Ardnacrusha dam by Siemens, and Ruston built LM175 the prototype Wagonmaster, the basis of all BNM's motive power since then.

Micheal Kennedy and Michael Portillo inspect the C&L on a newly recreated inspection cycle. This was based on an original design which worked over the C&L, nothing remained. We built it from scratch, it is very popular with visitors.

C&L

The future:

In terms of the most pressing projects our volunteers are busy relaying track so that the railway can operate public services after a long gap. A dedicated team of 4 volunteers work at weekends replacing sleepers and dog spikes with screws. Our Kerr Stuart 0-4-2T Brazil class loco "Dromad" remains in the UK awaiting an assessment on its boiler to be undertaken. All going well she will be back to Ireland after this work has been done, if funds can be sought it would allow Dromad and Nancy to steam together. This would allow two narrow gauge steam locos to be in steam together on a former CIE line in the Republic of Ireland, this last happened on the Cavan and Leitrim on 31st March 1959 and also since the County Donegal closed.

Attention is also focusing on the Tralee and Dingle Railway carriage collection. There are plans to restore former Tralee and Dingle Light Railway 3rd class carriage 10T to static display and to showcase her in the museum area. Also attention is focussing on TDLR, Bristol built 3rd class carriage 7T (dating from 1890). We have the necessary components to rebuild which include; the chassis of 7T, original TDLR bogies (from 8T), the original benches from 7T, and several recovered parts from other T&D Carriages. The most substantial item required is a replica body. When our volunteers can, additional accommodation will be sought and the chassis and bogies can be cleaned down and removed of surface rust so a full assessment can take place. Anyone who would like to contribute is asked to email us. This project would allow the C&L to have a very representative train of the Irish narrow gauge.

A project to fund both "Dromad" and 7T has been initiated it is known as the "C&L Vintage Train Appeal". It is very appropriate to fund both of these projects as Dromad has a T&D cab with cowcatchers, and the consist has the outline of what would be the Castlegregory branch train! Funding would be generously appreciated for this ambitious project. Those interested should make contact via Facebook or write to us.

Contact Details:

Address: Cavan and Leitrim Railway, Dromod Railway Station, Clooncolry, Co. Leitrim
Website: www.cavanandleitrim.com
Email:dromodrailway@gmail.com
Facebook: @Cavanandleitrimrailway

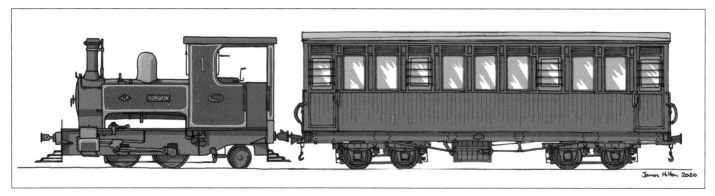

A commission showing our Vintage Train Appeal with Dromad and 7T paired together.

Darragh Connolly

C&L (Dromod) crest

Here we see 6T at Beturbet about to depart with a south bound goods from the transhipment platform, on 28th March 1959.

ARPT

Here we see 3T passing through Creagh en-route to Arigna. The steam locos often set fire to the neighbouring thatch cottages!

Bluebell Railway Museum Archive

Here we see 4L, formerly "Violet" passing the home signals of Ballinamore. Here the two single lines from Dromod and Arigna were side by side until the station

Bluebell Railway Museum Archive

5T lurks on shed at Ballinamore towards the end (note the missing cow catcher).

Copyright P. B. Whitehouse courtesy David Waldren

Here we see 6T at Mohill taking on water, note recently outshopped carriage 1L behind.

David Waldren Collection

6T en route from Dromod near Dereen in March 1959.

Here we see 4T showing her condition in colour, we see whispers of steam so she still has steam left in her.

The original C&L enamel sign at Ballinamore still standing after all this time, note the CIE poster to the right.

David Waldren Collection

4L slumbers at Ballinamoe shed, her condition is appalling.

David Waldren Collection

3T is seen being coaled from what looks like one of the ballast wagons, this was a very labour intensive process.

Ernie's Railway Archive

Nancy seen complete with her new brass dome, stands at the platform at Dromod like so many locos before her

C&L

3T has paused at Kiltubrid and is Ballinamore bound, note the condition of the carriage.

Colour Rail

Here we see 4T on shed at Ballinamore, she became possibly one of the grubbiest locos on the system towards the end.

Ernie's Railway Archive

6T approaches the platform at Dromod from Ballinamore on 16th March 1959.

David Waldren Collection

Kerr Stuart 4T is seen crossing the River Erne en-route to Ballinamore from Belturbet with bus coach 7L among the consist.

Ernie's Railway Archive

Belturbet to Dromod.
WEEK DAYS.

Sectional Running P	G	UP TRAINS	Mixed a.m.	Path for Coal Train a.m.	Path for Coal Train a.m.	Mixed p.m.	Mixed p.m.	Mixed p.m.
9	0	BELTURBET* w. ● dep. HALT	....	....	....	...	4 20	...
...	...	TOMKIN ROAD H N ,,	....	....	...	...	A	...
17	21	BALLYCONNELL* w. { arr.	....	....	...	...	4 40	...
...	...	,, { dep.					4 48	...
...	...	BALLYHEADY H N ,,	....	....	...	...	A	...
13	17	BAWNBOY ROAD* HALT { arr.					5 03	...
...	...	,, { dep.					5 08	...
...	...	KILLYRAN H N ,,					A	...
...	...	GARADICE H N ,,					5 19	...
16	20	BALLINAMORE* w. { arr.					5 30	...
...	...	,, { dep.	8 00	...	...	2 35	...	7 00
...	...	LAUDERDALE H N ,,	A	...	....	A	...	A
...	...	FENAGH H N ,,	A	...	....	A	...	A
...	...	ADOON H ,,	A	...	....	A	...	A
23	34	MOHILL* w. { arr	8 40	...	...	3 15	...	7 40
...	...	,, { dep.	8 50	...	...	3 25	...	7 50
...	...	DEREEN H ,,	A	...	....	A	...	A
16	22	DROMOD* ● arr.	9 11	...	...	3 45	...	8 10

Dromod to Belturbet.
WEEK DAYS.

From Dromod miles	DOWN TRAINS	Sectional Running P	G	Path for Coal Train a.m.	Path for Coal Train a.m.	Mixed p.m.	Mixed p.m.	Mixed p.m.
-	DROMOD w. dep.	0	0	...	...	12 20	4 50	8 40
2¼	DEREEN H ,,	...	...	...	....	A	A	A
5¾	MOHILL w. { arr.	16	21	...	...	12 40	5 10	9 00
	,, { dep.					12 50	5 15	9 05
10¼	ADOON H ,,					A	A	A
12¾	FENAGH H ,,					A	A	A
14¼	LAUDERDALE H ,,					A	A	A
16¼	BALLINAMORE w. { arr.	28	36	...	...	1 30	5 55	9 45
	,, { dep.					2 00	....	—
19¼	GARADICE H dep.					2 10	....	—
21¼	KILLYRAN H ,,					A		—
23	BAWNBOY ROAD HALT { arr.	14	18			2 20		—
	,, { dep.					2 25		—
24¾	BALLYHEADY H ,,					A		—
27¼	BALLYCONNELL W { arr.	11	14			2 40		—
	,, { dep.					3 00		—
30¼	TOMKIN ROAD H ,,					A		—
33¾	BELTURBET H arr.	16	20			3 20	....	—

A—Halt Stations. Trains stop when required to pick up and set down.
● Train Staff and Ticket Stations.

Ballinamore to Arigna.
WEEK DAYS.

From B'more miles	DOWN TRAINS	Sectional Running		Path for Coal Train a.m.	Path for Coal Train a.m.	Path for Coal Train a.m.	Mixed p.m.	Path for Coal Train p.m.
-	BALLINAMORE* ● dep.	0	0	...	...	...	1 50	...
3	BALLYDUFF H... { arr.	...	...	...	...	...	A	...
	,, ... { dep.						A	
3¾	CORNABRONE N ,,	...	...	...	...	...	A	...
7¼	ANNADALE N ,,	...	...	...	...	...	A	...
8¾	KILTUBRID { arr.	...	...	...	...	...	A	...
	,, { dep.						A	
10¼	CREAGH N ,,	...	...	...	...	...	A	...
12¼	DRUMSHANBO* + { arr.	54	56	...	...	...	2 48	...
	,, { dep.						2 58	
14¾	ARIGNA* ... arr.	10	16	...	...	...	3 15	...

Arigna to Ballinamore.
WEEK DAYS.

UP TRAINS	Sectional Running		Path for Coal Train a.m.	Path for Coal Train a.m.	Path for Coal Train a.m.	Mixed p.m.	Path for Coal Train p.m.
ARIGNA ● dep.	0	0	...	...	...	4 15	...
DRUMSHANBO W. + { arr.	12	18	...	...	...	4 33	...
,, { dep.						4 38	
CREAGH N ,,	...	...	...	...	...	A	...
KILTUBRID { arr.	...	...	...	...	...	A	...
,, { dep.						A	
ANNADALE N ,,	...	...	...	...	...	A	...
CORNABRONE N ,,	...	...	...	...	...	A	...
BALLYDUFF { arr.	...	...	...	...	...	A	...
,, { dep.						A	
BALLINAMORE arr.	50	56	...	...	...	5 35	...

For Speed Restrictions, see Page 209, Appendix to Working Time Table.
A.—Halt Stations. ● Train Staff and Ticket Stations.

The last C&L timetable, published in 1958.

Darragh Connolly

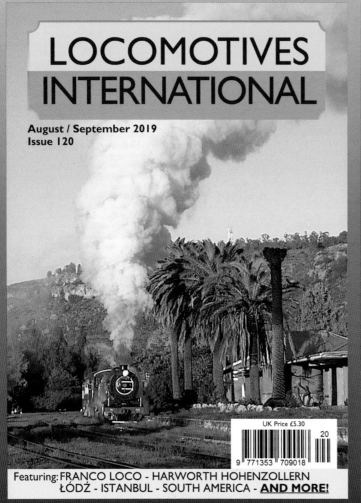